What Treat Can Ruben eat?

Story by

John-Ruben M. Aranton Jr.

Art by

El Tiburón Grande

AuthorHouse™
1663 Liberty Drive
Bloomington, IN 47403
www.authorhouse.com
Phone: 1-800-839-8640

Published by AuthorHouse 09/30/2015

ISBN: 978-1-4817-5376-0 (sc)
*   978-1-4817-5377-7 (e)*

Library of Congress Control Number: 2013908914

Print information available on the last page.

Any people depicted in stock imagery provided by Thinkstock are models,
and such images are being used for illustrative purposes only.
Certain stock imagery © Thinkstock.

This book is printed on acid-free paper.

Because of the dynamic nature of the Internet, any web addresses or links contained in this book may have changed
since publication and may no longer be valid. The views expressed in this work are solely those of the author and do not
necessarily reflect the views of the publisher, and the publisher hereby disclaims any responsibility for them.

authorHOUSE®

My Promise

In June 2008, my lovely daughter, Alessandra Kaylee, was born. I became a father who made a promise to always protect her. I knew that during her early years, she will depend on my wife and me for everything.

In July 2012, Kaylee had a severe allergic reaction to a pistachio nut. We knew she was severely allergic to dairy and eggs but not nuts. It was a traumatizing experience for me having to hold her tight as my wife administered the epipen. I was in tears as I continued telling Kaylee how sorry I was for not protecting her. It was the first time I felt I failed her as a father.

Four months later, Kaylee had another severe allergic reaction at daycare after accidentally drinking from another kid's cup that had milk. The teachers administered the epipen and called the ambulance. Waiting anxiously at the hospital, I recall seeing her carried into the ER on a stretcher with an oxygen mask. Her eyes were full of fear but suddenly changed to signs of comfort when she saw me. I failed her again!

After weeks passed, I continued working on this book, which I put on hold for years until the July incident. I realized no matter what I do, I cannot be by her side every minute. However by finishing this book, it will educate more people on the potential dangers of food allergies. With more awareness, it will provide a safer environment for my daughter and others.

To Kaylee, I dedicate this book to you! I will not always be there to protect you, but I hope this book will create a safer environment for you. I truly hope this fulfills the promise I made the day you were born. I love you!

What Treat
Can Ruben eat?

Deep in the woods,
lived Ruben the Raccoon.
He was wandering through the forest,
during the day around noon.

He saw Wesley the Weasel,
enjoying a light fare.
So, he walked over to him
to see if it's something he could share.

"No thanks, I'm not hungry.
Thanks for sharing your dish!"

So, Ruben kept walking,

"No thanks, I'm too scared.
The shell might give me a cut!"

Ruben scurried off.
His stomach growling LOUD!
He saw some friends eating.
So, he walked towards the crowd.

"Hey there, Ruben!"
Said Bernie the Bear.

"Would you like some berries?
There's plenty to share!"

His friends were all shocked.
They didn't know what to say.

When Ruben got home,
his stomach felt bad.

His mommy asked him,
"Why are you so sad?"

Ruben turned away. Feeling a bit shy.

His eyes started to water, he began to cry.

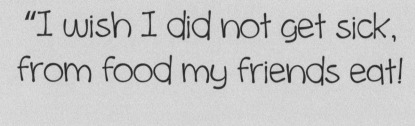

"I wish I did not get sick,
from food my friends eat!

I'm afraid they won't like me,
if I can't enjoy their treats."

Ruben's friends overheard him.
They came over to say,

I'm thankful for my friends…
Friends that always support me!"

Printed in the United States
by Baker & Taylor Publisher Services